David Dubinsky

A PICTORIAL BIOGRAPHY

Introducing a great American
to a great Czechoslovak diplomat
and Statesman, whose patriotic
leadership and unselfish, devoted
service to his nation will never be forgotten.

Respectfully,
Nicholas R. Marine
(Publisher)

NYC. 5/27/52

DAVID DUBINSKY

A PICTORIAL BIOGRAPHY

Text by JOHN DEWEY

Foreword by WILLIAM GREEN
Introduction by WALTER P. REUTHER

Published by
INTER-ALLIED PUBLICATIONS
New York, N. Y.

PRODUCED UNDER THE DIRECTION OF NICHOLAS G. BALINT
PICTORIAL PRESENTATION BY HARRY RUBENSTEIN
DESIGNED BY JOSEPH P. YAGO

———————

PRINTED IN THE UNITED STATES OF AMERICA
BY THE COMET PRESS, INC., NEW YORK, N. Y.

 65

DEDICATED

to the great army

of the men and women

whose industrial citizenship

in the ILGWU

has helped make

American democracy work.

Contents

TEXT

"David Dubinsky is a man of vision, integrity and courage."

HARRY S. TRUMAN

Foreword

PRESIDENT DAVID DUBINSKY of the International Ladies' Garment Workers' Union is outstanding in his devotion to the officers and members of the International Ladies' Garment Workers' Union, as well as to all other working people throughout the nation. Because of this fact, he is held in affectionate regard by the membership of the organized labor movement of the nation and by thousands of broad-minded, liberal, progressive people outside the ranks of labor.

President Dubinsky is uncompromising in his loyalty to and in defense of the economic philosophy upon which our great organized labor movement rests. No one can adequately appraise the value of the service he has rendered in the promotion of the economic, social and industrial interests of the membership of the International Ladies' Garment Workers' Union. President Dubinsky is honest, courageous, upright and is possessed of those characteristics which endear him to the hearts and minds of the membership of organized labor.

WILLIAM GREEN

Bezalel Dobniewski (1847-1934) of Lodz, Poland, father of "D.D."

Introduction

MEN OF STATURE, regardless of the level of society from which they spring, are marked by one common and enduring characteristic: They are essentially selfless souls, driven more by an undying inner urge to help humanity forward to a happier future than by the narrower impulse of personal ambition. I am proud of the opportunity to say that my long-time friend, David Dubinsky, fits honorably in this distinguished category.

But President David Dubinsky of the International Ladies' Garment Workers' Union is more than just my friend—he is the friend of every American who hungers for a fuller enjoyment of the fruits of democracy. His record of achievement, the deeds he has performed for the common good, stand out as the more singular for the fact that he had to surmount extraordinary obstacles to win the unquestioned esteem in which he is held by his fellow Americans.

He demonstrated his courage and his tenacity of purpose from the very beginning. Fighting the insufferable conditions of labor in the industry where he worked, daring to speak out for humanity's deeper hopes and promises, David Dubinsky proved his mettle by leading his people to immeasurable improvement of their working and living standards.

We of the UAW-CIO are particularly grateful to David Dubinsky for the hand of fellowship he extended to us in our own early struggles to organize our people for the fight against insecurity and indignity. Whenever the going was roughest, and the odds against us the greatest, David Dubinsky and the International Ladies' Garment Workers' Union always came through with timely assistance that helped us to win.

Few men in labor can match his contribution to the work of lifting the toilers of this land to a new and vaster appreciation of what democracy can do for people. His pioneering labors to broaden the functions of the labor movement have opened new horizons of progress to the workers of America. As one of the first men of labor to organize his people for the improvement not only of their physical but also their mental and cultural well-being, he breathed new life into the concept of a union with a spiritual conscience. From his work in this field has flowed a steady stream of experience and education, inspiring and helping workers in other unions to fashion new methods of joint endeavor for raising the levels of medical care, hospitalization and housing.

When historians come to weigh the worth of the great men of this crucial era in human history, I am certain that they will award David Dubinsky a high rank among the exemplary humanitarians of our time. In a period when the heart of mankind has caught an unforgettable glimpse of a world of peace and abundance and universal brotherhood, David Dubinsky is one of the hardest workers to keep that vision alive, feeding it tirelessly from his own bottomless spring of faith in the dignity of man.

That is his record, and it will stand against the years and decades to come.

WALTER P. REUTHER

DAVID DUBINSKY, MODERN LABOR LEADER

By John Dewey

IN 1908, a graduate of the University of Wisconsin started work for a degree of Doctor of Philosophy at Columbia University. He selected as the topic for his dissertation, "The Women Garment Workers of New York." In the first draft of his thesis he began to explain to the American public why these workers were unable to organize a strong labor union. They might be prevailed upon, he learnedly wrote, to fight on the barricades during a "revolutionary crisis," but they could hardly be expected, in any large numbers, to join unions, to attend union meetings, and regularly to pay their union dues. The day-to-day work of building a union and of correcting the thousands of petty worker's grievances would never appeal to their romantic spirits.

No sooner had this student begun to elaborate his thesis than the exploited workers in the needle trades took matters into their own hands, called general industry strikes, won concession after concession, and secured a permanent foothold in the trade union life of the city. The student dropped his dissertation, and went to other fields where the facts he had at hand made it possible for him to come to more valid conclusions.

Since those days, the unions in the women's garment industry have had their ups and downs, but during the last fifteen to twenty years have steadily increased in strength and

13

influence in the economic and political life of the nation.

Today the membership of the union embracing the women's garment industry — the International Ladies' Garment Workers' — is about 430,000. Its property, as represented in cash, bonds and welfare funds totals more than $100,000,000. It has advanced the living standards of its members from among the lowest to among the highest among comparable groups of workers in the country. It is operating a remarkably effective system for the settlement of industrial disputes. Its engineering department has made its mark on industrial efficiency. Its social welfare projects are a model for the nation. Its research, educational, recreational, and cultural activities are known and admired throughout the civilized world. In addition, it has been in the very vanguard of labor and civic forces in the battle for progressive labor and social legislation and for increased democracy in every aspect of our common life. And it has been, and is continuing to be, of invaluable service to the victims of oppression and the crusaders for democracy in scores of countries abroad.

Many thousands of men and women have contributed to the building of this great labor union. Since 1929, however, no one person has been more responsible for the union's remarkable development than has David Dubinsky, the General-Secretary-Treasurer of the ILGWU from 1929 to 1932, and its President since the significant campaign year of 1932.

David Dubinsky is a living example of the enrichment in spirit which America is continuously receiving from its immigrant population. From his early teens, Dubinsky has been a part and parcel of the organized labor movement. He was born in Brest-Litovsk, Russian Poland, on February 22, 1892, the youngest of six children. On reaching eleven, after some years of schooling, he went to work in his father's bakery shop. Three years later, in 1905, he became a master baker, and immediately joined the union. After a few weeks, he was elected assistant secretary, as one of the few members of the union who knew how to read, write and keep accounts.

In Russia this was a period of reaction. A year before occurred the abortive Russian Revolution of 1905, and workers' organizations were outlawed and many of their members terrorized and jailed. Young David was not an exception. Several times arrested for his union activity by the Russian police, he was finally sent to Siberia, but escaped, and later, in 1910, he was amnestied at the age of 18. The next year he decided to follow his brother Jacob to the United States.

Arriving in the States at the age of 19, young Dubinsky soon joined the Cutters Union Local Number 10, and worked at his trade for nearly a decade. After several years of activity in the Socialist and cooperative movements, Dubinsky, in 1916, became increasingly active in the Cutters Union, and in 1919 was elected its Vice-President and a year later, its President.

Under his leadership, the union took vigorous steps forward. The cutters secured a shorter work week and the administration was markedly improved.

In 1921 Dubinsky became the Local's General Manager and Secretary-Treasurer — a year when the union found itself the butt of attack by the cloak manufacturers' associations determined to reduce wages and return to piecework and the 48-hour week. The next year, he was elected a Vice-President of the organization.

In this capacity, during the twenties, Dubinsky joined

with President Benjamin Schlesinger, President Sigman and other leaders in the fight for democratic progress to ward off the attacks on the union launched by the anti-labor employers from without, and by the communists, with the rule and ruin policy, from within.

In 1929, on the resignation of Secretary Abraham Baroff, Dubinsky was elected Secretary-Treasurer. Three years later, on June 15, 1932, following the death of President Schlesinger, the General Executive Board elected David Dubinsky President of the Union.

When Dubinsky became President, the union was at a low ebb. Its membership was down to 45,000, less than half that of ten years before. The treasury was empty, and a host of creditors were knocking at the door. The personnel of the union had shrunk to seventy officers and forty clerks "who drew an occasional five or ten dollars when it was there to draw. At national headquarters the telephone service was sporadically discontinued and for days at a time one had to walk the stairs because the power was shut off. Visiting employers were told that the elevator was 'out of order.' The situation was as ludicrous as it was desperate."* Some of Dubinsky's fellow officers in fact thought the situation so desperate that ironically they congratulated the new President on his election as "undertaker."

But Dubinsky, a man of boundless energy and unquenchable optimism, put new spirit into the union. A few months after his election, Franklin D. Roosevelt was elected President of the United States, and the following year he inaugurated his "New Deal."

---

* Stolberg, "Tailor's Progress," p. 203.

Dubinsky and the entire union took advantage of the encouragement given by the section 7a of the Recovery Act which made it illegal for employers to oppose the organization of labor and outlawed the company union. The union began its first battle in the Philadelphia market, which, for over a decade, had been a notoriously open-shop town. To the surprise of the employers, the strike called by the union brought out ninety-five per cent of the dressmakers, and three days after it started was settled with a 10 per cent increase in wages, and with recognition of the unions.

The success of this strike had a profound effect on the International members throughout the country, and soon organizing campaigns were being pushed in 60 cities of the United States and in Canada.

In the meanwhile, the International was active in drafting a model code for the industry. At the code hearings in the cloak and suit trade in July, 1933, President Dubinsky headed a union delegation of which Morris Hillquit acted as the counsel.

Hillquit had previously been confined at his summer home in Belmar, New Jersey, a desperately sick man. On his sick bed he worked out a code which was destined to be a model for many of the industries of the country. He was flown in an ambulance plane to Washington and brilliantly presented the arguments for the union's draft.

The hearings lasted only two days. The code adopted embodied, for the most part, the union's suggestions. It provided for a 35-hour week and for adequate minimum wage rates for each craft. Organizing campaigns and strikes followed in the cloak and dress industry in New York and throughout the nation.

At the 1934 convention, President Dubinsky was able to report that the membership had increased from 45,000 to over 200,000; that the $1,000,000 indebtedness of 1932 had been liquidated, and that the union had assets of $850,000 — of which over a half million was in cash. Its progress to the present day, when the membership has reached two-fifths of a million and its assets are approaching $100,000,000, has been a steady one. Today, the ILGW Union is regarded not only as one of the largest and most powerful unions of the country, but a leader among organized labor in every branch of trade union activity and one of the most socially-visioned labor unions in the country.

On the occasion of a luncheon in his honor in recognition of his twenty years of activity as Executive Officer of the ILGWU, in April, 1949, the League for Industrial Democracy had this to say about President Dubinsky's leadership:

To DAVID DUBINSKY,
Secretary-Treasurer and President, International Ladies'
    Garment Workers' Union

"During the last twenty years you have served as Secretary-Treasurer, and for most of that period, President of the ILGWU. You have given the union the best of your great ability, rare common sense, constructive imagination and unflinching devotion.

"Under the inspiration of your leadership, and with the cooperation of its host of loyal officers and members the ILGWU has become one of the nation's most powerful and socially-visioned labor unions in this country. It has raised, to

18

a remarkable degree, the living standards of its members. It has helped to bring increasing order and efficiency into the industry. It has developed a sound and effective machinery for the settlement of disputes. It has been the implacable foe of racketeering, racial and religious discrimination, and totalitarianism of every type.

"Under your leadership, the ILGWU has become a pacemaker among American unions in the fields of health and welfare services, labor education, economic research, recreation, and the creative arts. It has vitally contributed to political action and community undertakings in behalf of the social advance. It has given unstinting moral and financial support to the fighters for human liberty in every portion of the globe.

"While playing a monumental part in the above achievements of the ILGWU, you have contributed much outside the union to countless causes for the public good.

"In recognition of your past services to the Union, to America and to the world community, the League for Industrial Democracy, an educational organization dedicated to 'increasing democracy in our economic, political and cultural life,' expresses its deep gratitude to you, and wishes you Godspeed in all your future activities for a better world in the difficult and challenging days ahead."

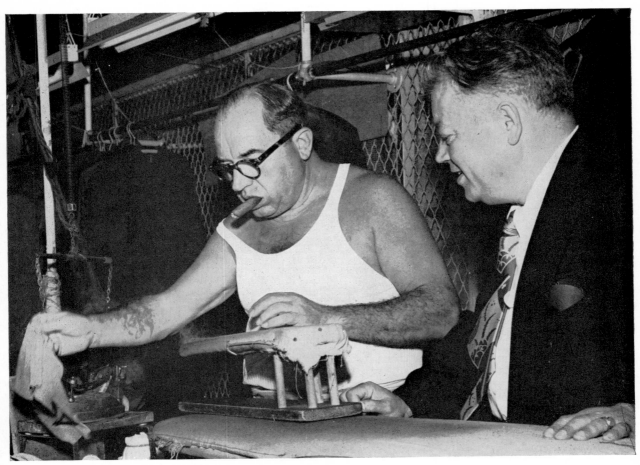

Frequently "D.D." visits one of the garment plants on "The Avenue." Here he is quizzing the "ironmaster."

DAVID DUBINSKY: MASTER CRAFTSMAN OF LABOR

ONE of the most engaging and influential figures on the American national scene today is David Dubinsky, president and secretary-treasurer of the International Ladies' Garment Workers' Union.

"D. D.," as his more intimate associates like to call him, arrived in America a youngster of 19, by slow stages, from a West Siberian camp for political exiles, an assignment he had earned at the age of 15 as strike leader in a bakery shop owned by his father in the city of Lodz, Poland, at that time part of the empire of the Czars.

His baggage as he reached the port of New York consisted chiefly of rugged health and a personality bubbling over with inexhaustible energy and restless enterprise which even a turbulent and bitter adolescence and long months in prison could not dim or mar. Twenty-one years later, "D. D." took over the presidency of an ILGWU tottering from the effects of the debacle of the early 30's and of an internecine war induced by Communist aggression, and fashioned it into a great union, a pace-maker in the field of collective bargaining, of widespread welfare benefits and, what's equally significant, a pathfinder in the area of world-wide aid to struggling free trade unionism everywhere.

From 1900 to 1932

It would be unfair, as well as inaccurate, to state that the ILGWU today reflects in its entirety the handiwork of David Dubinsky. Born in 1900, the union of the women's garment workers had capable and inspiring leadership before Dubinsky assumed its presidency in June, 1932, following the sudden death of Benjamin Schlesinger in a Colorado sanatorium. The ILGWU had a stormy career for more than three decades prior to the "Dubinsky era," and those years served as a school of "hard knocks" for tens of thousands of cloakmakers and dressmakers, and bred cadres of tough and experienced trade unionists.

It is, nevertheless, indisputable that the new ILGWU of today, though resting upon the core of the old battalions, is chiefly the creature of David Dubinsky whose courage, vision and innate genius for organization and for welding "areas of union strength" together has forged a unique labor union out of an inchoate mass of workers, women workers largely, who for a great many years were regarded as unorganizable by students of the trade union movement and even by active partisans in the ranks of organized labor.

Architect of Union Strength

In this job of fluid social architecture, David Dubinsky has displayed extraordinary talents and he has applied them in that direction to the hilt. A union, it need be observed, is never static; it is, by its very nature, a dynamic body, functioning in malleable environs and subject to constant change, adaptation, development, or decline. The assets of a successful union are not necessarily the amount of money it collects in dues or the size of treasury it possesses. It is rather such intangibles as membership cohesion, a growing sense of material security, the spiritual vigor emanating from improved standards of living, the zest of extra-curricular activity, the impact of collective influence on legislation, and, finally, industry-mindedness, which offer the safest yardstick of union strength. For along with these intangibles comes the more tangible evidence of union power—high membership rolls, the contractual guarantees of work terms, educational and informational publications, intra-industry welfare agencies, and alert, active union staffs.

A Labor "Financier"

As labor leader, "D. D." has occasionally been described as a paradox, largely because of the many-sided and often clashing aspects of his personality. Resourceful and adroit in building his union's enviable financial structure, it is pointed out, Dubinsky is as prudent as any good business man in handling the distribution of his union's funds. He insists on getting utmost value for every authorized dollar of expenditure. There's no frittering away or careless throwing around of union dollars.

In point of fact, "D.D." is singularly proud of his adroitness as a union financier, of his well-earned reputation as the "watchdog" of the union's treasury. He came up, it will be remembered, as secretary-treasurer of the ILGWU in a period of the union's leanest days. Yet, "D. D." is very well known among his associates not only as a warm-hearted person, to a point of sentimentality, but as one who plans and thinks far in advance of the union's far-flung contributions to labor and philanthropic causes, at home and abroad.

What sort of man is David Dubinsky in relation to the men he works with—his general executive board and his district directors outside and in New York, where the main, old-line strength of the ILGWU resides?

General Plus Staff

"D. D." is no John L. Lewis or any similar labor chieftain who congenitally cannot suffer differences of opinions from lieutenants or "cabinet members." He likes quick decisions and he has a lot of faith in his own judgment, yet he is careful to consult with his vice presidents even in situations where he least expects disagreement. He believes in sharing his responsibilities with his top board if only for the emotional satisfaction he derives from that. On the other hand, Dubinsky would be the first to admit that he owes his major achievements, those which have gained for him over the years the respect of friends and foes alike, to the loyal help and unquestioning cooperation of his hardworking and alert "general staff."

Years of exercise of authority and the inescapable awareness of his present stature in the general American community have, beyond cavil, wrought material changes in David Dubinsky's personal attributes since the day he first hit New York City as a wide-eyed youth 40 years ago. He has acquired poise, self-confidence, and what is usually referred to as dignity. Yet, it seems that he is not afraid to "risk" this dignity on occasion by unconventional behavior even in public. It is not uncommon, for instance, to observe "D. D." at conventions of his huge union, in the presence of 1,000 delegates, or at any other large ILGWU assembly, personally attempt to reshuffle chairs and benches as if he were faced with an alarming shortage of manual help on the platform.

Direct Yet Flexible

Dubinsky frankly takes pleasure in the good things of life, yet this compactly built, high-tensioned human powerhouse still is unfamiliar with the arts of true relaxation. There are a few other men in the labor movement who may equal but not exceed him in the passionate, driving force he applies to his daily schedule. Sympathetic, with a smile occasionally wrinkling his keen face, he is, nevertheless, frequently given to sharp repartee bordering on bluster. Still, despite trigger-quick explosiveness, Dubinsky is capable of highly disciplined maneuvering and is a fine hand at diplomacy which serves to smooth his path toward an objective. Direct in his methods yet flexible, "D. D." will strive to avoid head-on collisions in dealing with the "party of the second part" in the belief that a more subtle approach will produce the results he is seeking without deadlocking issues or creating hopeless stalemates.

His Social Philosophy

David Dubinsky is thought of by many people, and probably regards himself, as a doer rather than a thinker or theoretician. The truth, or the sounder appraisal, of course, lies somewhere midway between these two points. Dubinsky is a doer, all right, as his hard-hitting, indomitable fighting qualities will reveal. From his earliest years, however, Dubinsky has absorbed a laborite philosophy with a heavy socialist coloration grounded in a solid trade union base. From varied experiences of a tough career, in later years he has acquired a code of conduct which is neither pure idealism nor 100 per cent sophistication, but partakes of the nature of both. He does not like to pose as a "man of the people" with attendant "ground-roots," homey trimmings, but his thinking seldom takes him away from hard realities which appear to suit snugly his bearing and temper.

If pressed for a direct reply, the ILGWU president would, in all likelihood, be ready to admit that he is guided by the principle that realism is the only workable idealism. He obviously regards union leadership as a trusteeship and himself as the most dependable trustee his union could have possibly chosen. Few will disagree that he is eminently fitted to stay on as president as long as his health and age permit, even though such certainty may jar some sensitive concepts on the subject of office tenure. Fact of the matter is, union presidencies in the labor movement are rarely, if ever, challenged with regard to consistency of self-succession. Unions, much less than any other of our social institutions, are worried about limiting office tenures, as long as they consider their top officers capable, honest and loyal.

Passion for "Trail Blazing"

It is fair to state that "D. D." has himself been as much stamped with the "personality" of the ILGWU, as the union is being indelibly fashioned in his mould. At the union's recent semi-centennial convention in Atlantic City, President Dubinsky, in his opening speech, cited "22 firsts" in every conceivable social and economic area of action which the ILGWU has initiated in the past five decades, most of them miles in advance of any other union in the country. A great many of these "firsts," his audience well knew, had been initiated and realized thanks to his ingenuity and vision. Yet, his own identity with the union he leads is so deeply rooted that the uninitiated present inside the Convention Hall that morning would hardly have suspected that the major credit for these achievements really belonged to "D. D." When he spoke from that platform in terms of "we," one felt in his every word unalloyed pride and a sense of total inseverability from the organization of which he was only a part, though its chief spokesman.

The great majority of the employers in the women's garment industry—an industry with an annual production output of nearly five billion dollars—are not intimidated by the ILGWU president, despite the union's tight control over working conditions. Barring occasional clashes with individual firms, chiefly in the newer markets, the ILGWU has encountered no cause for calling major strikes since the early days of the New Deal, depending solely on collective bargaining and impartial machinery for ironing out wage, hour and welfare benefit differences.

"Industry-Mindedness"

This "miracle" of industrial peace, of course, is not a heaven-sent gift, nor is it the result of a special climate pervading the garment industry, in contrast to other trades or industries. It is based on what the ILGWU president often refers to as "industry-mindedness," a concept which most of the garment employers share with the union and which has required decades to take root. The idea that "a prosperous union cannot exist within a sick or profitless industry" has been merged with the thought that "industry cannot prosper in an atmosphere of labor strife and low work conditions" and found effectively coordinated and working. And few men in the American labor movement have toiled harder for the promotion and the realization of this inter-dependence of interests than David Dubinsky.

"Give and Take" in Community Life

The hard row which trade unionism has had to hoe in America for more than a century has been imbedded as much in employer opposition, judicial obstruction and governmental hostility as in its rejection by wide and varied community segments with their base lodged chiefly in the middle economic groups.

To a large degree, this antipathy has been the fault of the unions themselves which chose to function as a "state within a state," living apart from community needs and interests. This trade union apathy toward community life, however, has undergone a radical change in many unions in recent years. And the ILGWU, under the inspiration of David Dubinsky, has made a major contribution in that direction.

Today, it may truthfully be stated, there's not a social, philanthropic or humane movement, on national, city or town levels, in which the home office of the ILGWU or its locals from coast to coast are not taking an active part. Dubinsky has actually built up cooperation with community into an ILGWU policy, urging union aid and union interest in every community affair, large or small.

That this co-living with community life has paid off in helping to dissolve or soften antagonisms toward trade unions, in the smaller towns in particular, is an accepted fact. It is one of the main pillars of ILGWU prestige today, David Dubinsky believes, this two-way pattern of union practice—of giving as well as taking.

"D. D." at Home

Judged by common standards, the bustling, super-energetic ILGWU president is a "homebody" who prefers a few hours of rest on the terrace of his apartment on the 20th floor of the Chelsea Corners residential "skyscraper" in the company of his small family to any extra-mural diversions.

Dubinsky, who spends his energy lavishly during long workdays chockful of conferences, meetings and consultations with his staff, depends on these rest periods at home as his only effective recuperative medium and he amazes his co-workers by the rapidity with which he regains working momentum. His only outdoor relaxation used to be bicycling, an exercise in which he engages less and less frequently with the years. Cigar smoking is another "vice" which he is eternally trying to shed without much success.

He and his wife Emma have one daughter and a five-year-old granddaughter who live in the same building. Little Rina is the apple of her granddaddy's eye and the sparkplug of every morsel of juvenile joy and mischief in the Dubinsky menage.

The ILGWU's "Marshall Plan"

Dubinsky, it has been told, is not particularly fond of the term "labor statesman," partly because it is frequently applied with an undertone of concession, if not of empty flattery. He prefers to be known for what he is—a union president and a first-rank organizer of labor.

He has been honored lavishly by kings, presidents, by foremost civic leaders, and by men and women of the labor movement, and he has learned to accept these honors with grace and tact, though he may not be overly fond of the ceremonial side of it. David Dubinsky is not a philanthropist—in fact, he was raised in an atmosphere where charity was looked at askance as the product of a disordered and inequitable social order. Yet, this labor union president has initiated in the past fifteen years a relief movement among the members of his own organization—for war sufferers and Fascist victims—which has netted nearly 20 million dollars, distributed in a manner that has gained for him and for his ILGWU universal admiration and untold blessings. This has been, in fact, the ILGWU's own pre-Marshall "Marshall Plan."

Key Figure in Free Labor

The ILGWU, during the twenty years of its direction by David Dubinsky, has not been merely watching history in the making. Under his guidance, the economic well-being of nearly a half million workers in a highly competitive and mercurial industry has been brought up to match and overtake earnings and work conditions in many other older organized American industries. In the past four years, Dubinsky has been the key figure in a global campaign for the promotion and acceptance of the free-labor concept of democracy. In his own AFL, David Dubinsky has been one of the bold initiators of a very effective movement to encourage, through organization and by material and moral support, the formation of free trade unions in Europe and Asia.

This, then, is a thumbnail portrait of an amazing man at the top rung of labor's ladder who got there through sheer mastery of the magic of human organization against almost insuperable odds: ex-prisoner of the Czar and trusted friend of presidents; a unique and pioneering figure in the world of today, a fervent devotee of democracy, and still young enough to be heard from on a grand scale in the years to come.

A long line of distinguished Americans and dignitaries as well as plain folks from abroad sent their tribute to David Dubinsky and the League for Industrial Democracy. The President of the United States sent the following letter:

28

April 14, 1949

Dear Dr. Dewey:

Please extend my hearty greetings and sincere good wishes to all members and guests attending the forty-fourth annual conference of the League for Industrial Democracy.

In honoring Mr. David Dubinsky, who has served the International Ladies Garment Workers Union as its president for twenty years, I feel that you do more than felicitate one man. David Dubinsky is a man of vision, integrity and courage. I feel that he, too, will value the testimonial to him as recognition of the valiant work of many thousands of working men and women of this country who, while seeking to advance their mutual interests, have served the democratic well-being of their country. His career is a living witness of the forward progress of collective bargaining through a score of years.

I wish you every success for constructive service in carrying out the theme of your program today, "Democratic Planning for Security with Freedom." Liberty-loving Americans know that security without freedom is totalitarian, and freedom without security is false.

Very sincerely yours,

Harry Truman

Dr. John Dewey,
Honorary President,
League for Industrial Democracy, Inc.,
112 East 19th Street,
New York 3, N. Y.

THE STORY THE CAMERA TELLS

I. *Youth to Maturity*

This old photo shows the courtyard of the "Labor College" in Lodz, Poland, the political prison of that big textile city, "Class of 1908." The inmates, jailed striking members of the Lodz Clerks' Union (white collar workers), are having their allotted fresh-air half-hour under the argus eyes of jailer Captain Egorev. (Captain Egorev, "D.D." says, was a venal barbarian whose hand had to be constantly "greased" by the "politicals.")

Boyhood days in Lodz, Poland.   Youthful "D.D.," in first formal photo.

"When life was young, utterly young . . ." This early photo shows "D.D.," barely out of his teens, picnicking with friends somewhere in the Jersey Palisades.

35

Top: Mastering cutting skills.
Bottom: "D.D." at his youthful best.

Bedecked in loose Sunday linens, smiling out on a world he sets out to "conquer."

"D.D." is ready for his bike ride—the only outdoor activity he indulges in—
cycling through crowded West Side streets on many a Sunday morning.

II. *Leading the Union*

"D.D." leads "Operation Union" in New York's great dress industry in the summer of 1933, which ushers in new era of stabilized peace in that industry. Following walkout of 60,000, employers agree to collective peace pact. Left to right: Alfred W. Lasher, employer representative; Grover Whalen, former police commissioner, and "D.D."

David and Emma, at the closing hour of the ILGWU's 1937 "seaside" convention, in a happy mood as that conclave registers the unbroken march of the union's progress. "It seems we both picked the best man," Mrs. Dubinsky told the audience as she was called by the chair to take a bow.

Top: "D.D."—in the fall of 1937—relaxes briefly at Atlantic City. With him are the late Sidney Hillman, president of the Amalgamated Clothing Workers, and Jacob Potofsky, then ACWA's general secretary.
Bottom: In the fall of 1938, the top command of the ILGWU at a meeting in Washington decided to withdraw from the CIO. Photo shows "D.D." discussing with his publicity director, Max D. Danish, the statement announcing this withdrawal.

Top: "D.D.'s" press staff, representing ILGWU's English, Italian, Jewish and Spanish publications, circa 1938. Seated are: Harry Crone, "D.D.," Max D. Danish, Simon Farber. Standing are: Serafino Romualdi, Herman Wolf, Harry Rubenstein, Vanni B. Montana and Antonio Reina.

Bottom: "D.D.," flanked by members of the cast, cuts birthday cake as "Pins and Needles," ILGWU hit revue and Broadway's darling show, passes its second year of "Standing Room Only" in the fall of 1939, at Labor Stage playhouse.

William Green, AFL prexy, welcomes ILGWU back to the "House of Labor" at its 1940 Convention in Carnegie Hall, New York City. "D.D." is overjoyed as old charter is returned to Ladies' Garment Workers.

Top: "D.D." discussing with A. Philip Randolph, president of Brotherhood of Pullman Car Porters (AFL), strategy for Congressional action on a Permanent Fair Employment Practices Commission.
Bottom: "D.D." meets the press. The ILGWU chief is at his best dissecting problems of garment industry and parrying knotty questions by newsmen.

Top: A midsummer afternoon scene at Unity House on a Sunday morning, 1942. The late Jan Valtine, author of "Out of the Night," is describing his escapes successively from the tentacles of Nazism and Communism to a spellbound audience. "D.D." is seen on lower left.

Bottom: A bevy of girl delegates invade the platform of the 1944 Boston convention as the tellers announce the re-election of "D.D" by acclamation.

Top: "D.D." standing on right presents new "Impartial Chairman" of New York's coat and suit industry, Harry Hopkins, confidant of the late President Franklin D. Roosevelt. Standing left to right are: Charles Baker, Israel Feinberg, ILGWU vice president, Samuel Klein, Max Zuckerman, Joseph L. Dubow, employer executives. Seated are, left to right: James J. (Jimmy) Walker, ex-mayor of New York, and Mr. Hopkins, who succeeded Walker on September 6, 1945. Hopkins died a few months later.
Bottom: "Dave" meets "John," the great labor maverick, at President Truman's Labor-Management confab in October, 1945, and both swap some unrecorded impressions . . .

"March of Time" shows up in February 1947 with a garment documentary—
"Fashion Means Business." This photo shows the ILGWU chief in conference
with Executive Secretary Frederick F. Umhey while Hannah Haskel Kreindler,
"D.D.'s" talented secretary, and Siemon Hamburger, general auditor, lend an ear.

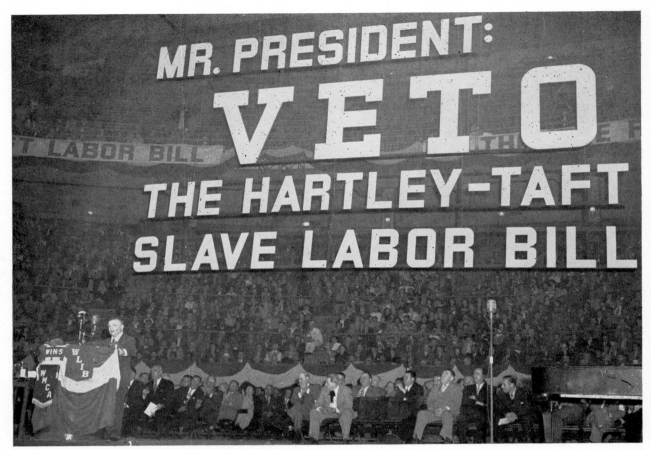

At rally in Madison Square Garden, New York, May 4, 1947 organized labor, 25,000 strong, urged President Truman to veto the Taft-Hartley Act. "D.D." is seen addressing the huge audience.

Appearing before the Senate Labor sub-committee in 1947, "D.D." opposes the Taft ban on industry-wide collective bargaining and the closed shop.

"D.D." calls on ILGWU affiliates to give material aid to automobile strikers in the fall of 1947. On the stage of New York's Manhattan Center, United Auto Workers' president Walter P. Reuther, flanked by "D.D." and film star Melvyn Douglas, waves a cluster of checks totaling $97,000 donated by ILGWU locals. Former U. S. Senator Robert M. LaFollette, Jr., is at left.

Top: Years of officerhood have not dulled his skills. On a recent visit to the big Barbizon slip plant in Paterson, N. J., "D.D." exhibits his deft handling of the cutting machine as Barbizon officers—left to right: Ben Weiss, general manager, Gerald Ritter, president—and some union officers look on.

Bottom: Triennial balloting in Cutters' Union, Local 10, "D.D.'s" alma mater, is a "must" democratic chore for all—great and small. "D.D." casts his ballot.

Top: Year after year "D.D." plays host at Unity House to scores of employers from the various industry associations. The scene above catches the "bosses" in a burlesque demonstration serenading "D.D." and chanting "Will You Love Us on Seventh Avenue as You Do at Unity House?"

Bottom: "D.D." personally distributes tickets in New York's garment center for Truman election rally organized by Liberal Party at Madison Square Garden on October 27, 1948.

Top: With Secretary of Labor Tobin, Federal Security Administrator Ewing, U. S. Senator Lehman and AFL President Green smiling on him, "D.D." samples some of ILGWU's Health Center's radiology as he ranges himself for chest examination behind an X-ray machine.

Bottom: "D.D." in pleasant chat with fellow craftsmen in "Cutters' Corner" on New York's Seventh Avenue.

Sixty-five thousand dressmakers stopped work on the morning of May 12, 1949 to follow the hearse which bore the body of William Lurye, ILGWU organizer slain while on active duty by assassins hired by labor's enemies. Heading the throng of mourners as hearse moves down Seventh Avenue is "D.D.," followed by the union's General Executive Board.

Another link in the ILGWU health-center chain is forged as "D.D.," in May, 1949, receives "key" to new Wilkes-Barre, Pa. Health Center. Looking on, from left to right, are: Philip Kramer, vice president; Dr. Albert Feinberg, medical director; Adolph Held, health and welfare director; Frederick F. Umhey, executive secretary, and vice president David Gingold, director of Northeast Department.

"D.D.," with ever-present cigar in hand, is leafing through a volume of "personal history," covering the twenty years of his presidency, compiled by his secretary, Hannah Haskel Kreindler.

"D.D." and his "General Staff," 1947-1950. Clockwise from left are: Charles Kreindler, Philip Kramer, Louis Levy (deceased), Meyer Perlstein, Louis Stulberg, Morris Bialis, George Rubin, Jennie Matyas, Charles S. Zimmerman, Hannah Haskel Kreindler, secretary to "D.D."; Julius Hochman, Israel Feinberg, Frederick F. Umhey, "D.D.," Luigi Antonini, Max D. Danish, editor of "Justice"; Joseph Breslaw, Salvatore Ninfo, Isidore Nagler, Max Cohen (deceased), Harry Wander (deceased), Samuel Otto, John S. Martin, Edward Molisani, David Gingold, Harry Greenberg and Benjamin Kaplan.

"D.D." brings down the gavel as union's Golden Jubilee Convention—at Atlantic City, May 23, 1950—gets under way.

III. *In the National Arena*

"Command Performance" of "Pins and Needles," in East Room, White House, March 3, 1938, with the late President Franklin D. Roosevelt prominently displaying show's playbill. "D.D." and the cast are beaming happily.

Top: The late Wendell Willkie, who swept meteor-like the American political skies in 1940, stressing a point which the ILGWU chief palpably enjoys . . .
Bottom: ILGWU's Labor Stage in Times Square area was remodeled during World War II into a servicemen's canteen.

"D.D." presents a "Victory Ambulance" to AFL vice president Matthew Woll
for transmission to the front during World War II. The money was raised by
members of locals affiliated with the New York Cloak Joint Board, ILGWU.
Vice presidents Israel Feinberg and Joseph Breslaw look on.

"D.D." in the very thick of the Roosevelt-Truman Campaign in 1944. Left to right: Dr. John L. Childs, state chairman of the Liberal Party; Alex Rose, chairman of the state administrative committee, and "D.D." at huge Liberal Party rally in New York. The then Senator Harry S. Truman points to Liberal line on registration poster.

One of a half-dozen "Liberty Ships" built with funds realized from war bond purchases by ILGWU members and earmarked for that purpose during the war years—1942-45—glides down the runways at Baltimore into Chesapeake Bay. "D.D." is in the lower center with several associates, among them vice presidents Nagler, Feinberg, Zimmerman, Rubin and Kreindler, and Nathaniel M. Minkoff, secretary-treasurer of the Joint Board Dress and Waistmakers' Union.

Top: A girl member is initiated by "D.D." into the ILGWU Health Brigade during World War II.
Bottom: Lieut. Gen. Mark Wayne Clark, on his way to receive the Four Freedoms Award from the Italian American Labor Council, stops over at the ILGWU offices in New York City for a visit with "D.D."

ILGWU marks 65th anniversary of Franklin D. Roosevelt's birthday with presentation of bust in granite by noted sculptor Gleb W. Derujinsky. Bust was unveiled January 13, 1947, with impressive ceremony at entrance to Roosevelt Memorial Library, Hyde Park, in presence of members of Roosevelt family. "D.D." and Mrs. Roosevelt shake hands while son Elliot and Faye Emerson look on.

Presidential family applauds famous entertainers at Madison Square Garden where on October 27, 1948 the memorable windup meeting of the presidential campaign took place. Left to right are: Margaret Truman, Mrs. Truman, the President and "D.D."

"D.D." meets Elder Statesman Bernard M. Baruch at the opening ceremonies of the expanded Union Health Center, 275 Seventh Avenue, New York City, February, 1949.

"D.D." offers Franklin D. Roosevelt, Jr., ILGWU and Liberal Party support in special Congressional election in New York 20th District in the spring of 1949. AFL president William Green on left.

At the 1949 annual luncheon of the League for Industrial Democracy where "D.D." was guest of honor. Left to right are: Dr. Harry W. Laidler, executive director of LID, "D.D.," Gordon R. Clapp, chairman of Tennessee Valley Authority, and Thomas C. Douglas, Labor-Socialist Premier of Saskatchewan, Canada.

Top: A staunch supporter of Americans for Democratic Action (ADA) from its formation, "D.D." is seen on speakers' dais at ADA's traditional Roosevelt Day Dinner in 1949 at the Hotel Astor in New York City. Applauding Mrs. Roosevelt, from left to right, are: U. S. Senator Hubert Humphrey, FDR's biographer Robert E. Sherwood, and former Secretary of the Treasury Henry Morgenthau, Jr. *Bottom:* The League for Industrial Democracy, at its 44th Annual Conference, April 23, 1949, presented a citation to "D.D.," "one of the greatest labor leaders in the country." "D.D." responded by urging "alliance of labor and intellectuals" for social progress. AFL president William Green is seen displaying citation to gathering. 70

ILGWU's FM radio station WFDR was inaugurated at a gala ceremony at Carnegie Hall in New York on June 16, 1949. Among the guest speakers were, left to right: General Walter Bedell Smith, former Ambassador to Moscow, "D.D." and General David Sarnoff, head of the Radio Corporation of America.

Edward Arnold, Hollywood's best-known "laborite," visits with "D.D." prior to attending Carnegie Hall dedication of ILGWU's FM radio station, WFDR, in New York City, June 16, 1949. Frederick F. Umhey, union's executive secretary, on left.

"D.D." forecasts victory for former New York Governor Herbert H. Lehman in latter's race for U. S. senator in the fall of 1949.

Thousands at outdoor rally supporting Liberal Party's candidate for Mayor of New York City, Newbold Morris, in the fall of 1949. "D.D." is introducing Morris who is standing on sideline near platform.

Top: The 90th birthday of Professor John Dewey provided a unique opportunity to his multitude of friends and admirers to pay him richly earned tribute. "D.D." extends congratulations to the leader whose life and works have influenced modern education more than that of any other single man. William H. Kilpatrick, Professor Emeritus of Education, Columbia University, is in the center.
Bottom: At Gompers' Centennial dinner-meeting, January, 1950, in Washington. Left to right are: Vice president Alben Barkley, Mrs. Barkley, "D.D." and AFL president William Green.

"D.D." endorses the 1950 United Negro College Fund and pledges support by ILGWU at luncheon at the University Club of New York. Left to right are: John D. Rockefeller, Jr., chairman of the National Council of the Fund, Winthrop W. Aldrich, chairman of the board of Chase National Bank.

Eddie Cantor flew in from the West Coast to take part in the ILGWU "Convention Jamboree" at Atlantic City, May, 1950. What "D.D." tells him as he firmly grips his hand will remain a Cantor secret.

Top: "D.D." offers Nelson Rockefeller some background stuff of "With These Hands," ILGWU's documentary film, following its premiere at the Gotham Theatre, Times Square, June, 1950. Director Jack Arnold is in center.
Bottom: "D.D." applauds salient point by Senator Paul H. Douglas of Illinois, main speaker at political rally of New York Local 22 on Oct. 25, 1950. Local manager Charles S. Zimmerman at right.

"D.D." receiving honorary degree of Doctor of Laws from James H. Case, Jr.,
president of Bard College, Annandale-on-the-Hudson, New York, June 16, 1951.

IV. *For A Free World*

"D.D.," former President Herbert Hoover, and AFL vice president Matthew Woll at luncheon meeting, in the fall of 1940, called to protest Stalin's invasion of Finland.

The late Mayor Fiorello LaGuardia auctioning off paintings by members of Local 22, New York Dressmakers, on October 21, 1942, in the Ferargil Galleries on East 57th Street. Watching the "auctioneer," left to right, were: Charles S. Zimmerman, vice president of ILGWU; F. H. Wood of wartime China Relief Agency, beneficiary of the auction and "D.D."

Photo exhibit arranged through the initiative of ILGWU in May, 1945, displays
scenes of Nazi barbarities in the Warsaw Ghetto. Left to right: AFL vice president
Matthew Woll, William Wolpert, Governor Thomas E. Dewey, Mrs. Fiorello
LaGuardia, the late Mayor Fiorello LaGuardia, and "D.D."

"D.D." receives million-dollar check from Dr. Israel Goldstein, on behalf of the State of Israel, in repayment of a one-year loan made by ILGWU to Israel in June, 1948. "Israel's credit is tops," ILGWU chief comments.

Top: At the dedication on July 15, 1948, of ORT trade school building at Montreuil, near Paris, set up with funds contributed by ILGWU. Left to right are: Daniel Mayer, former French Minister of Labor; Jefferson Caffery, U. S. Ambassador to France; "D.D.," and the late Leon Blum, three times Socialist premier of France.

Bottom: "D.D." on the way toward Mondello, seashore suburb of Palermo, Italy, to open up officially the Roosevelt Institute of Maritime Arts—organized and maintained by the ILGWU—where hundreds of war orphans are learning the skills and trades of the sea. "D.D." is seen in company of (left to right) Mrs. Bruno Buozzi, leader of school; Cardinal Ruffini, Archbishop of Palermo; Signor Avolio, the Mayor of Palermo, and Mrs. Dubinsky. The date: July 24, 1948.

Luigi Nardi, Italian Consul General in New York, pins on "D.D." the "Star of Italian Solidarity"—"in recognition of ILGWU's contribution to relief and democratic reconstruction" in that country. The date: October 19, 1948.

"D.D.," AFL secretary-treasurer George Meany, AFL president William Green, and George M. Harrison, president of Railway Mail and Steamship Clerks' Brotherhood, as they depart on board of "Ile de France" November 19, 1949, to help found the International Confederation of Free Trade Unions.

Top: "Clothes for Needy Tots" in five European countries. "D.D.," surrounded by officers of Local 105 and leaders of juvenile coat employers' associations, spurs labor-management effort in children's apparel industry to send thousands of child garments abroad to clothe the little boys and girls still destitute and needy in the DP camps. From left to right: Charles Baker, executive director, Infants' and Children's Coat Association, Inc.; Adolf Held, director of Welfare and Benefits, ILGWU; Martin Cohen, manager of Local 105, ILGWU; "D.D.," Henry Rothman, president of Infants' and Children's Coat Association, and Carl Stone, president of Infants' and Children's Sportswear and Novelty Association.

Bottom: Leaders of the Congress of Industrial Organizations and of the American Federation of Labor are in London to attend the International Confederation of Free Trade Unions. Strolling within the shadow of Parliament are "D.D.," William Green, Allan Haywood and Martin Kyne, both of CIO; Jay Lovestone, and Henry Rutz of AFL staff.

This moment of high emotion occurred at the Golden Jubilee Convention of the ILGWU at Atlantic City, as one of the five orphan "ambassadors," a junior student at the Mondello Institute near Palermo, sent from Europe to offer thanks for the union's generosity, fairly leaped on the ILGWU President with a bouquet of flowers clutched in one little hand.

Mourning the death of Leon Blum, Labor and Socialist leader of France. Seated in speakers' row on platform in Manhattan Center are, left to right: "D.D.," Warren R. Austin, former U. S. Senator and chief of United States delegation at United Nations, and Alexander Kahn, general manager of the "Daily Forward."

"D.D.," prime mover in the Amun-Israeli Housing Corporation's 1951 drive for $10,000,000, in executive session with leaders of the project. Seated from left to right are: Jacob S. Potofsky, president of the Amalgamated Clothing Workers of America; Charles H. Silver, president of American Woolen Company; Nelson Rockefeller, and "D.D." Standing left to right are: Anna Rosenberg, Assistant Secretary of Defense; Isador Lubin, representing Israel; Charles S. Zimmerman, ILGWU vice president, and Louis Hollander of the Amalgamated.

V.   *With His Family*

Rina—a major soft spot in "D.D.'s" bosom—on a visit to Grandpa's office.

Dancing with Jean, his only child, "D.D." palpably enjoys the gay steps on the floor of Unity House, where she, not he, obviously is the leader.

"Sunday in the Park." The three Dubinsky generations make up a vivid group on a cool and sunny Sunday morning in Washington Square Park, in New York's lower Fifth Avenue.